FINISHING LINE PRESS

www.finishinglinepress.com

Hail, Radiant Star!
Seven Medievalist Poets

poems edited by
Jane Beal, PhD

poems by
Jane Beal
Gail Ivy Berlin
Albrecht Classen
Thom Foy
Katharine Jager
A.J. Odasso
Katherine Durham Oldmixon (Garza)

Finishing Line Press
Georgetown, Kentucky

Hail, Radiant Star!
Seven Medievalist Poets

ACKNOWLEDGMENTS

Some poems in this anthology were previously published:

Jane Beal
"Medieval Bestiary Poems: 'Kyrios,' 'Light,' 'Star,' 'Unicorn,' 'Pelican,' 'Lamb,' 'Phoenix,' 'Lion,' 'Logos,'" *Integrité: A Journal of Faith and Learning* 17:2 (Fall 2018), 77-80.

Katharine Jager
"Recuperation and Recitation: The General Prologue," *The Gettysburg Review* 22:3 (Autumn, 2009), 482-83.

Katherine Durham Oldmixon (Garza)
"How to Make a Palimpsest Before it Was a Metaphor," *Cider Press Review* (Fall/Winter 2013).
"Photographs of the Saint's Finger Are Strictly Prohibited," *Bellevue Literary Review* (Spring 2011).
"Tonantzin, La Guadalupe de Juan Diego" and "Marina, La Malinche," qarrtsiluni (Summer 2010).

The cover image for this book is "The Polar Star" by William Shackleton (1872-1933). The image is in the public domain and freely available here:

https://www.the-athenaeum.org/art/full.php?ID=250002

The editor wishes to express her thanks to each of the poets who so generously and creatively contributed their poems to this volume as well as to the fine folks at Finishing Line Press for choosing, publishing, and promoting this book.

Publisher: Leah Maines
FLP Editor: Christen Kincaid
Cover Art: *Polar Star* by William Shackleton
Cover Design: Elizabeth Maines McCleavy

Printed in the USA on acid-free paper.
Order online: www.finishinglinepress.com
 also available on amazon.com

Author inquiries and mail orders:
Finishing Line Press
P. O. Box 1626
Georgetown, Kentucky 40324
U. S. A.

Table of Contents

Thom Foy

Katharine Jager

A.J. Odasso

Katherine Durham Oldmixon (Garza)

For our readers

*May your hearts be filled
with starlight!*

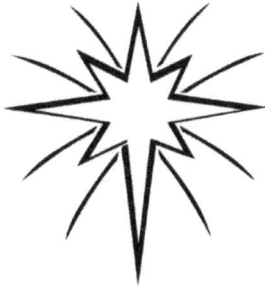

*Heyl, excellent princes, Mary most pure!
Heyl, radiant sterre, the Sunne not so bryth!
Heyl, Moder of Mercy and mayde most mure!
The blessyng that God yaf Jacob upon you now lyth.*

Hail, excellent princess, Mary most pure!
Hail, radiant star, for even the sun is not so bright!
Hail, mother of mercy and maid most demure!
The blessing that God gave Jacob is now upon you.

From the *Ludus Coventriae*
or "The Play Called Corpus Christi"

(c. 1475)

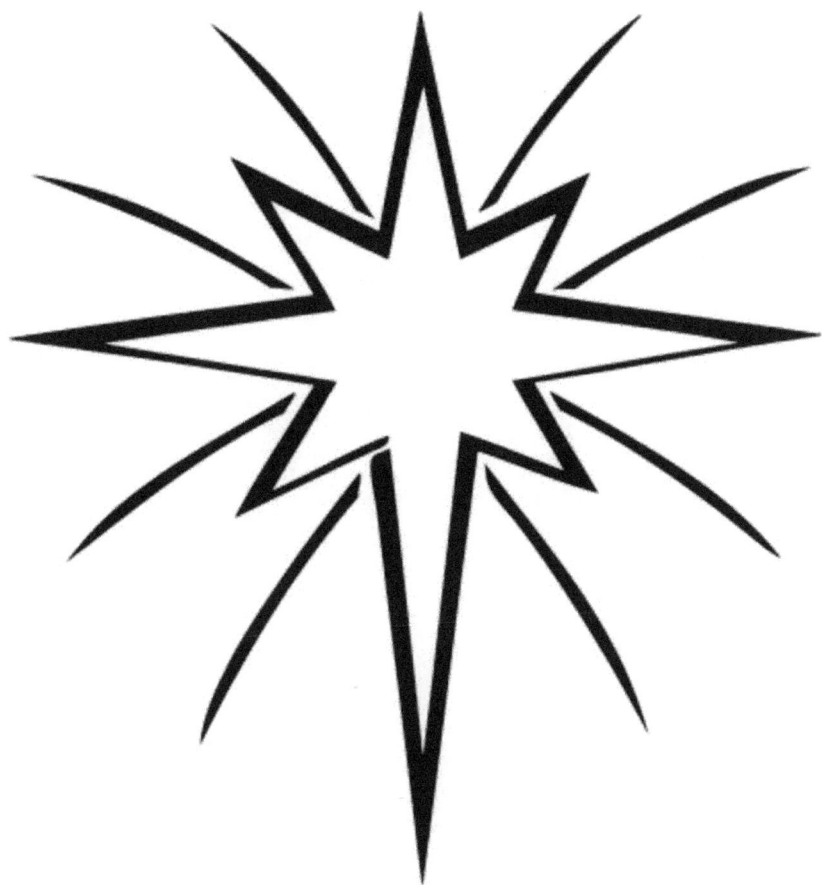

INTRODUCTION

Of Stars and Starlight,
the Middle Ages and Contemporary Poetry

Beginning several years back, a group of poets, who were also medievalists, would gather together to read poetry at the International Congress on Medieval Studies, which is held annually in May at Western Michigan University in Kalamazoo, Michigan. We read our poems to one another in a somewhat informal, *ad hoc* way. These poetry readings generally took place in the late afternoon, during one of the "wine hours" sponsored by publishers at the Congress, where the mead (a honey-fermented drink) might draw in passersby to listen. Our pleasant exchanges—poets reading to "a fit audience, though few" (as post-medieval poet John Milton once put it)—eventually developed into something slightly more formal: we proposed our poetry readings as sessions to be included in the official Congress program. Much to our surprise and delight, our proposals were accepted, included, and publicized to our fellow medievalists, more of whom began coming to the "medievalist poetry" readings.

As we had before, we continued to offer the "open mic" feature (admittedly almost always without an actual microphone), so anyone who came could read poetry, too. Naturally, this included poetry original to the participating medievalists but also poetry in the original languages of the Middle Ages (Latin, Old English, Old French, Middle High German, Middle English, and so on) as well as faithful or free translations from those original languages. This led to much learning and merriment for all who participated. Because, of course, there are different epistemologies, different "ways of knowing," the Middle Ages, its literatures and its cultures. The experience needn't be all dusty manuscripts in dark libraries! (Though actually, I should quickly say, that's what draws many of us to the field, being the strange creatures that we are). At these International Congress on Medieval Studies sessions, there were some memorable moments and some remarkable performances.

I, for one, learned more about Reynard the Fox, a sly but delightful creature whom I had met before in Chaucer's *Canterbury Tales* and *Sir Gawain and the Green Knight*, in the fables of Marie de France (where he is nameless) and in the folktales of Uncle Remus' (where he is re-named "Brer Fox"). But now I considered him anew, specifically because he was transported from a medieval world into a modern one in contemporary poems read at these sessions by medievalist Oz Hardwick. So later, when I saw a red fox in the green grass by the side of a road in the Midwest, I felt moved to write my own little poem about Reynard. Then, when I taught about the fox in my college literature courses, it was with a sharper awareness of his character and influence. This is only one example of how I became both more inspired and better educated by participating in these readings—and I was not the only one who so benefitted.

Eventually these poetry sessions sparked a bright idea in one of our best colleagues, the very same Oz Hardwick who knows so much about Reynard. He realized (to invoke Walter Ong) that all this orality—namely, our medievalist "poetry out loud" readings and performances—ought to be paired with some literacy, or rather, paired with a tangible artifact for the literate, so that we might preserve the memory of what we had shared. That is, we ought to make a book and see about getting it published! The idea of an anthology of medievalist poetry was an attractive one. Most of us were supportive of the idea, and quite ready to contribute poems to such a book, but some of us secretly had little hope that it would be published or garner any attention at all. How would we tempt a publisher to invest ...? We enthusiastically went along with Oz's plans anyway. This proved all to the good.

In 2015, Stairwell Books, a small independent literary press in York, England, published our first anthology: *New Crops from Old Fields: Eight Medievalist Poets*. The book received favorable reviews in popular blogsites that had a readership interested in the intersection of the Middle Ages and contemporary poetry. Julie Chappelle's lively review in "Medievally Speaking" is a stand-out example of one of these. She kindly concluded of our work that "the 'old fields' of medieval literature and history lovingly plowed and sewn with fresh seeds by modern poets have engendered delightful and inspiring 'new crops' that will refresh any who partake of these evocative, powerful, and revealing [poems]." Certainly, refreshment is a great gift to anyone in this day and age (as were Chappelle's encouraging words to us).

The anthologized "medievalist poets" went on to give a series of readings from our new book, coordinated by Jane Chance, professor emerita of Rice University, which were held at the International Congress on Medieval Studies in Michigan, the International Medieval Congress in Leeds, England, and the meeting of the Modern Language Association, which was held in Austin, Texas that year. These were open to everyone, and included other medievalist poets who came to read as well, and so the circle of readers and writers widened. We took copies of our books on the road with us to our own readings, performances, and shows to entertain other listeners. In short, we celebrated "medievalist poetry" in a variety of academic and not-so-academic settings in the U.S.A. and England.

These small victories led to a sense that there ought to be a sequel to the first anthology. The title of the first collection came from some lines of Chaucer's *Parliament of Fowles*:

> For out of olde feldes, as men seith,
> Cometh al this new corn from yeer to yeer:
> And out of olde bookes, in good faith,
> Cometh al this new science that men lere.

> (For out of old fields, as men say,
> comes all these new crops from year to year;
> and out of old books, in good faith,
> comes all this new knowledge that men learn.)

This title conveyed a central theme of our book and the experiences that led to its making. So in turning to the creation of a second volume, I looked to follow the model already set.

Symbolism of the Star

Like New Crops from Old Fields, the title, *Hail, Radiant Star!*, is a modernization of some lines of Middle English poetry found in a play, "The Play Called Corpus Christi" (c. 1475):

> *Heyl, excellent princes, Mary most pure!*
> *Heyl, radiant sterre, the Sunne not so bryth!*
> *Heyl, Moder of Mercy and mayde most mure!*
> *The blessyng that God yaf Jacob upon you now lyth.*

> (Hail, excellent princess, Mary most pure!
> Hail, radiant star, for even the sun is not so bright!
> Hail, mother of mercy and maid most demure!
> The blessing that God gave Jacob is now upon you.)

The Virgin Mary was often praised in effusively bright, devotional terms in late-medieval literature and culture, as she is in this quatrain. It was common to call her, in Latin, *stella Maris* or "star of the Sea"—for there is a pun between the Englished Hebrew name "Mary" (from Mirriam) and the Latin noun, "mar, maris," which means "the Sea." In English, like Latin, Mary was also looked upon as a "radiant sterre."

The star was a powerful symbol in the Middle Ages, and it could stand for more than one idea. Given the extensive influence of the Bible, a star could remind medieval readers or listeners of Queen Esther (whose name means "star"), or the Star of David, or the Star of Bethlehem. It could call to mind a verse from the second epistle of Peter, in which Peter speaks of Jesus as the "Morning Star" (2 Peter 2:1), or a verse from Revelation, in which Jesus, in a vision to John on Patmos, says he will give "the morning star" to the one who "is victorious and does my will to the end" (Revelation 2:28). On the darker side of biblical star-symbolism, the king of Babylon was also called "the morning star" (Isaiah 14:12). In later medieval thought, this was linked with a passage from Luke 10:18, "I saw Satan fall like lightening from heaven." So the epithet "the morning star" became associated with the devil, also called Lucifer. Medieval people were warned against being deceived by his light.

Given the influence of Greco-Roman mythology, a star also could remind medieval readers and listeners of Venus, the planet called both "the morning star" and "the evening star" in classical literature, after the Goddess of Love. The star symbol might also remind medieval people of the stars in the constellations—like Ariadne's Crown or Orion's belt—or any of the twelve signs of the zodiac, for most of them saw Astrology, like Nature, as a hand-maiden of God. Indeed, educated medieval people imagined a Ptolomaic universe in which there was a sphere of fixed stars, the *Stellatum,* and the music of the spheres was singing throughout the cosmos. It is to and through this sphere of the fixed stars that Dante imagines himself journeying in *Paradiso*, the third book of his *Divine Comedy*, and Chaucer uses the motif himself in his *Troilus and Criseyde* and *House of Fame*.

The journey to the stars appears again much later in the 20th century work of a famous medievalist poet, J.R.R. Tolkien. In his poems and his prose *Silmarillion*, Tolkien tells the tale of Eärendil, who traveled in his ship the Foamflower with a shining, pearlescent Silmaril bound on his brow. In the heavens, Eärendil took his place by the will of the Valar. So in Tolkien's mythology, the morning star is actually that Silmaril shining down on Middle-earth.

Considered from a modern point of view, just as from a medieval one, the star is a versatile symbol. Think of the "North Star," Polaris, the brightest star in the constellation Ursa Minor ("Little Bear"). People speak of "following the North Star" because people actually use it for navigation. Interestingly, modern astronomers have shown that the "North Star" is actually two stars in close orbit. Yet poets and singers today sometimes speak of "following the North Star" in a metaphorical sense, meaning they are following that which they love or value most—a lover, a mother, God. Rascal Flats has a 2004 country song in which they declare, "Every long-lost dream led me to where you are / And others who broke my heart, they were like northern stars / Pointing me on my ways into your loving arms / This much I know is true: / God blessed the broken road that led me straight to you." Not only the North Star, but other stars are used in this sense of guiding the poet to love. In a 1989 duet, Prince and Sheena Easton sing, "The arms of Orion / that's where I want to be / Since you've been gone / I've been searching for a lover in the sea of tranquility / drowning without you, my dear ..."

The star seemed an appropriate symbol to invoke in the title of this poetry collection, *Hail, Radiant Star!*, for, in a sense, there are many stars within it. Only two poets included actually use the word "star" directly: Katherine Durham Oldmixon (Garza) writes in her poem, "Tonantzín, La Guadalupe de Juan Diego," of how the Virgin Mary "wears / a veil of stars on a Mexican-blue sky" (ll. 1-2), and I (Jane Beal) ask of the literal star in the title of my poem, "Star," about the Morning Star, Jesus: "does the morning star / rise in your heart / as a little child sings / her lullaby? / That star does not fall ..." (ll. 3-7). Other poets use words that include "star" within them—"starting," "stared," "starling," "*starf*," "Starbucks," "starved"—but more significantly, the symbolic ideas embodied in the star, in both medieval and modern times, are hidden in their poems. This collection is a *microcosmos*, and each poem in it is like a star: light shines from them, like, I hope, the light of wisdom in a dark place.

Starlight from Seven Constellations

There are seven poets who have written poems to light up the little universe of the book: Gail Berlin, Albrecht Classen, Thom Foy, Katharine Jager, A.J. Odasso, Katherine Durham Oldmixon (Garza), and me. Each poet has contributed a group of nine poems, and in reading and re-reading these verses, I have discerned themes that unify each group like constellations that are connected by stars in the night sky. So I introduce each poet's group of nine poems in terms of the constellation it recalls to my mind.

Like the other poets here, I (**Jane Beal**), an associate professor at the University of La Verne in southern California, have a constellation for our readers, my "constellation of Corona Borealis" poems. In classical mythology, the crown was made by the Smith-God, Hephaestus, for Ariadne of Crete on her wedding day to the god Dionysus and later set among the other stars in the sky. Neither Ariadne nor Dionysius ever appear directly in my constellation, but they are there, especially in the first poem, "Kyrios," which pictures the menageries of Cirque du Soleil in their steampunk show "KURIOS: Cabinet of Curiosities" and the movie, "The Greatest Showman." The poems that follow are like pages torn from a medieval bestiary, but specifically those pages on which a creature or created thing is allegorically interpreted to stand for some quality of Jesus, the Incarnate God. In "Light," birds fly like a "living crown" around the tree; in "Star," the eyes of the baby Jesus are full of light! In "Unicorn," I recall the Incarnation; in "Pelican," the Crucifixion; in "Phoenix," the Resurrection. "Logos" considers IHS, the medieval monogram for Jesus. The contrast between the last pair of poems, "Lamb" and "Lion," highlights the difference between the God-Man who willingly sacrifices himself for the world and the God-King who powerfully resurrects himself—and then awakens his lion-cubs from the sleep of death.

Gail Berlin, a professor of English recently retired from Indiana University of Pennsylvania, has given us the "constellation of Lyra" poems. Lyra is named for the lyre of Orpheus, and like Orphic songs, the poems Berlin shares have an elegiac quality of mourning to them. They recognize different kinds of losses—"a true grail" that can't be seen directly, "a winch" in another kingdom, a friend who died—so that now, as she says in "Another Sort of Time," the "dark waters lift the fullness of the lily." Her poems invoke strange medieval myths, as in "Shapeshifter," and stranger stone carvings, as in "Sheela Na Gig," that haunt readers with the sense that something is missing—or hidden. Yet there's hope for what comes in the future when remembering what's come in the past, in the final poem, "River Enough." In it, Berlin writes, "I can hold my space—I can overflow it: / I've danced out of my slippers / —lots of times." Grails, winches, lilies, rivers, and slippers are all powerful images in Berlin's poems, like an image from "How to Change" with which her constellation began: "a kite without wind has nothing / to lose." After so many losses, there may be nothing more to lose. A kite in such a case is no longer *doing* something, it is *being* something—something, indeed, that is beautiful.

Albrecht Classen, University Distinguished Professor of German Studies at the University of Arizona, shows us the "constellation of Pegasus." When Pegasus, a white horse with wings, was born, he flew to Mount Helicon and befriended the Muses. He made a spring of waters (*pegai* means "waters" in Greek) called the Hippocrene, meaning "the horse's fountain." If anyone drank from it, he was blessed with the gift of poetry-writing. The mystically-minded speaker of Classen's poems has drunk from this spring. In "Dawn," the first poem in Classen's constellation, we are introduced to this restless dreamer. In "The Crane," he experiences the touch of a silver bird's wings on his eyes while he is sleeping and is "reborn."

In "Mysticism," he reflects on the matriarchs of the medieval mystical tradition—Hildegard, Mechthild, Catherine, Bridget—and the way they challenged "male concepts / about God." In "Kalamazoo," Classen's speaker contrasts the academic study of the mystics with a poignant question: "Margery's tears continue to flow / —how do we respond to her cries?" In "I, the Foreigner" and "Medieval Individual," he reflects on aspects of identity. Nearly every poem in this constellation contains a reference to dreams, and in the poem "Our Dream," Classen writes of the passage of life itself as a kind of dream. In "At Night"—a long, thin poem—Classen gives us a cascade of images, especially in the concluding stanza, as if from a dream: "pearls," "corals," and "clouds / among the leaves / and deeply in the sea." In "Unnamed," Classen reminds us that the "sugar of life / results / from our pain." The last word of the poem is "light."

Thom Foy, a teacher of writing and rhetoric at the University of Michigan, Dearborn, has the "constellation of Leo" poems. The Greeks named this constellation after the Nemean lion, which Hercules slew, and it contains a star, called Regulus, that the Babylonians called "the star that stands at the Lion's breast" or "the King Star." Foy (whose name means "faith" in French) reveals this star. His constellation begins with two poems about love between romantic lovers, which are followed by two poems about love at Christmas, that concern familial love. The fifth poem, "Transgression," meditates on the subject of its title with the metaphor of the poet looking at his younger self through the "wrong end of a telescope." This is the heart of the constellation, for there are four stars on either side of it. It is a dark heart, but even so, its wisdom illuminates. On the other side of it, in "The Quiet King" and "Sweltering: Two Views," Foy returns to meditations on divine things: one on the "still, small voice" (1 Kings 19:11-13) and the other on Alpha and the Omega (cf. Revelation 22:13). The last two poems, "The Tender" and "The Ease of a Sunday Walk in Winter," evoke the beauty of nature. Foy writes in "The Tender":

> He watched the clouds and heard them speak.
> He saw birds come in and out of his mind.
> He felt wisdom in its place and easy. (ll. 4-6)

Reading these lines, I was reminded of Bede's story in *The Ecclesiastical History of the English People,* told by a king's man, of the sparrow that flew in and out of a window: he compared it to our life, flying from one winter into the next, so that we do not know where it is coming from or where it is going—until we know God.

Katharine Jager, associate professor of English at the University of Houston-Downtown, shares with us the "constellation of Carina" poems. Carina means "the keel," as in the keel of a ship, and that constellation was imagined to be the keel of the ship Argo Navis, the ship that Jason and the Argonauts sailed on their quest to obtain the Golden Fleece. Jager's poems are questing poems that direct her readers to a point. She shows us what poems can do with medieval allusions: describe real birds with the accuracy of an ornithologist ("Recuperation and Recitation: The General Prologue"), demand we pay attention to domestic violence in communities that won't ("Legenda Aurea"), and defend women who choose to wear the hijab ("Varieties of Religious Experience"). Bestiaries, saints' legends, and the Song of Songs are sources of influence for her creativity, as "Scent and Bestiary," "The Dragon" (Saint Margaret's, that is), and "For the Markaris (after Palestrina)" clearly show. She pushes past medieval metaphor in "Renaissance Technology" but returns to it in "Iona," which recalls "Columba, / little dove of Christ, your heart each morning / turned to face the dawn."

A.J. Odasso, medievalist and poet-extraordinaire, splits our attention in the "constellation of Gemini" poems. Gemini stands in the sky for the twins, Castor and Pollux, who had twin sisters, too, Helen and Clytemnestra. In some myth-versions, the twin-pairs were Castor and Helen, and Pollux and Clytemnestra. In all versions, Castor's father was divine, and Pollux's father was human. When Pollux died, he asked to share his immortality with his brother, and this was granted. Like the initials of the poet's first name, A.J.'s poems in this collection are of two kinds: some, a medievalist's poems; some, a poet's lyrics, with hardly any medievalism discernable in them at all. In the latter category are "Prosthetics," "DNR," and "Timepiece," each expressing different kinds of pain: "Timepiece" remembers a father who left; "DNR," a great-grandmother who died of consumption. In "Prosthetics," the speaker whispers, "my twin scars ache." In the former category are "Cruel Sister, Revised," which takes inspiration from the Child Ballads, and "Two Recto Fragments," in which the speaker addresses two pages from a French prayer-book (dated to ca. 1410). Four poems bridge the two categories in terms of imagery and themes: "Origin Story," "The Breakers Fail," "Haunting Harvard Square," and "Treasure." These imagine monsters and remember ghosts.

Katherine Durham Oldmixon (Garza), Professor of English at Huston-Tillotson University in Austin, Texas, shines through her "constellation of Virgo" poems. In classical mythology, the Virgo of the constellation stood for the Greek Goddess of Justice, the daughter of Astraeus, father of the stars, and Eos, goddess of the dawn. Virgo stands in the night-sky near Libra, the constellation that represents the scales of justice. In like manner, Oldmixon is just in her poems, seeking the right balance from the beginning of her constellation of poems. There she quotes the Old English elegy, "The Seafarer," in modern English translation: "May I for my own self song's truth reckon." Her opening poem, "Crossing," investigates the emotional reality of border-crossing from Mexico into the U.S., but in terms so metaphoric and universal that readers understand "crossing" in a cosmic way: a journey of the soul.

She also includes saints' poems about St. Teresa of Avila, St. Agatha (patroness of volcanoes, bell makers, bread bakers, and nurses), and St. Sebastian; all three poems are ekphrastic explorations, too. Long after Ovid, she ventriloquizes Philomela, and long after what has been called "the discovery of the new world," she speaks in the voice of Marina, "La Malinche," the woman who was sold as a slave to Hernán Cortés, the conquistador. Marina was his translator, and she bore his first son, Martín, the first mestizo in the Americas. Oldmixon writes poignantly from her point of view, "I would hold my tongue, but must speak / to survive. My father sold me destined to lie / with a man who crossed our oceans to let blood / and tongues mingle. I keen lullabies." Of course, Oldmixon's constellation is also Virgo because of her poem in honor of the Virgin Mary, already mentioned, "Tonantzín, La Guadalupe de Juan Diego." In it, she writes, "Her scent brought / a bishop to his knees. Yet they say

/ a woman is no god, only a human / sanctified by maternity ..."

There are eighty-eight constellations in the night sky. In the *microcosmos* of *Hail, Radiant Star!,* there are only seven: the Crown, the Lyre, the Pegasus, the Lion, the Ship's Keel, the Twins, and the Virgin. Yet hopefully there is enough light from them to brighten a reader's heart.

Jane Beal, PhD
Casita Amber Ridge
June 2018 / rev. May 2019

CODA:

A Star on a Shield

Famously, in the Middle English Arthurian romance called *Sir Gawain and the Green Knight*, the device on Gawain's shield is a pentangle—in the shape of a star—and it is attributed to King Solomon, famous for his wisdom. The poet tells readers that it betokens "trawÞe": truth, troth, fidelity. Its five points represent five virtues that, when practiced together, demonstrate fidelity: *fraunchyse* (generosity), *felaȝschyp* (fellowship), *clannes* (cleanness, purity or chastity), *cortaysye* (courtesy), and *pité* (mercy). These, too, are part of the star symbolism inherited in the present from the medieval past. The star on Gawain's shield, the poet adds, is called "the endless knot."

For more on stars, see http://www.constellation-guide.com/.

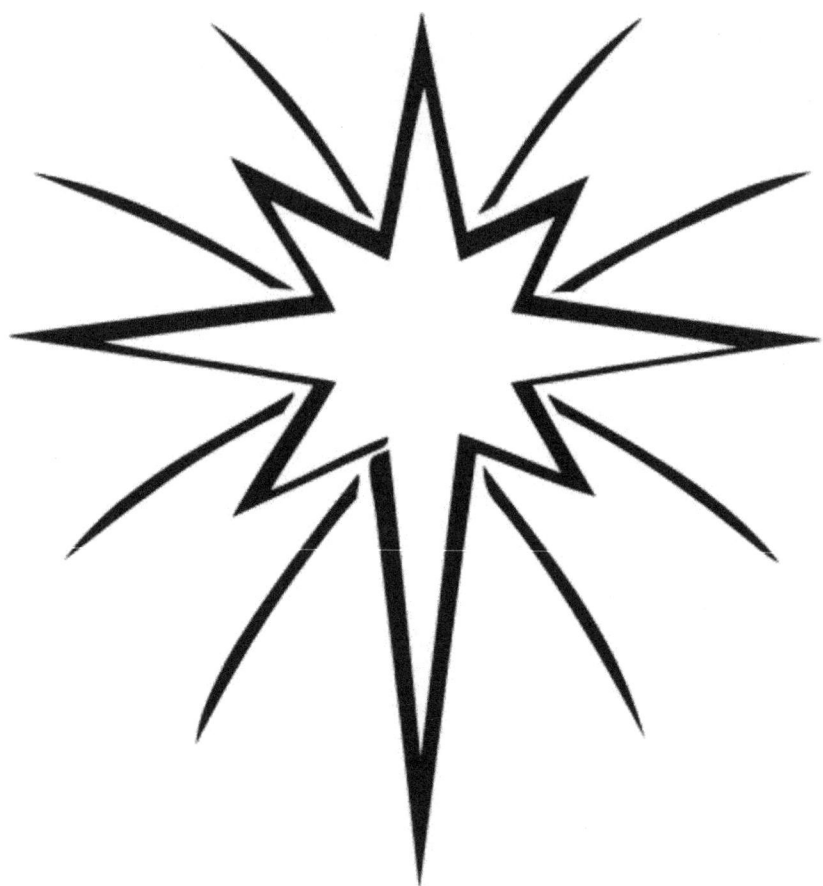

JANE BEAL

Kyrios

Kyrios, I'm curious—
did I hear you right
in the dark?

Cirque du soleil,
and the cabinet of curiosities,
is still spinning in a lost memory in my mind ...

But now, the little boy is dancing
with the little girl, casting light with the lantern
on the wall, dreaming and singing

of a future better than the past:
will you embrace them,
will you embrace us?

Kyrios! Kyrios! I reach out my hand
toward the light from your Star,
as I behold the circus animals in the ring

all of them roaring—lion, lamb, unicorn,
pelican and phoenix, bursting into flames—
as a red cardinal transforms into a parrot

and the valley of peace is pierced
by the beak of my lover's soul, fearful
and yearning for our embrace, our

embrace, dear Lord! Have mercy,
Kyrie eleison, Christe eleison—
his mouth is so sweet against my mouth.

Kyrios, I'm curious—
did I hear you right
in the dark?

Light

I.

I look into the tree: it is white at the core.
Innocence or emptiness? Death or waiting?

The whiteness reaches down deep,
but the roots of the tree are deeper.

The whiteness reaches up high,
but the branches of the tree are higher.

II.

The birds fly in and out of the thick leaves
like a living crown around the tree: a dove

perches above them all. The bright sun shines
on her shimmering breast and folded wings.

She is singing, in her way: story-telling, truth-telling,
telling the life of her glorious soul-tree.

III.

The light is shining on the leaves!
The light is illuminating what is invisible.

As I watch, a golden resin, like a new sap, begins
to flow up through the roots that were injured

into the white core of that beautiful tree,
making it even more

alive.

Star

Dazzling in the dark,
sparkling like diamond—

does the morning star
rise in your heart

as a little child sings
her lullaby?

That star does not fall,
but shoots across the sky,

then hovers over a stable
in the House of Bread

where the maid-become-mother
rocks the baby in her arms.

His eyes are full
of her starlight,

reflecting time and eternity
and the love in her face,

with the fearlessness he inherited
from heaven.

Unicorn

The tender scene, so beautiful in the forest,
when the maiden sits in the middle of the path that runs
through the trees, and the unicorn lays his head in her lap:

Incarnation of God! What magic is in the world?
The hunters draw closer, but still, you lie at peace
like a newborn baby wrapped in swaddling clothes

and laid in a manger. The woman with you cannot
imagine how the sword will pierce
her own heart, too.

Pelican

I find you on the world-map:
an image of avian motherhood.

You bow your head, you pierce your breast,
and your blood feeds three little ones.

Christ! Of course this is a picture
of your Crucifixion.

Lamb

The Lamb stands on a stone altar.
We do not have to bind him.

Blood pours out from his sacred heart
through a wide, wet wound where he was pierced

into a golden chalice: drink this blood.
The life is in the blood.

Phoenix

My Phoenix wouldn't be false—
this, the Resurrection of God!

Flaming fire, blazing bright,
casting shadows in the night!

But my little phoenix is the memory
of pain. What does this bird do? Looks
ugly, worming up from the ashes, fleshy,
then downy, moulting, edging
out her wings, flapping in the mess
of a nest, growing, growing, growing—
what power! terror! sorrow! misery!
Then suddenly, those two wings open
gloriously, like a double-rainbow
in the desert, beautiful before an invisible hand
crucifies them on the cross-beam, so that
screaming in pain, she burns as she turns
    incandescent:

flaming fire, blazing bright,
casting shadows in the night!

O Phoenix! My little resurrected phoenix-soul
is weeping ruby-tears for all the years.
Begin again: renew. In the dark,
holy beloved, be true.

Lion

The stone lion shakes his mane
and comes to life!

He leaps into love, roaring,
so that the cubs awaken.

They lift their sleepy heads, resurrected,
and open their eyes to the Promise.

Logos

The Logos is a whisper
I hear in the silence.

My word echoes the Word:
everything that is written

is written for our instruction.
O sacred name! This, IHS.

Gail Ivy Berlin

How to Change

I am starting with a bowl of milk
I will not drink, or a woolly mammoth
emerging from ice, or wisteria seeds
in a drawer by the sink: I am not sure what
I should be today, beyond a strong sense
of needing to move
away from the fledgling impaled on the thorn, away
from the map or the ledge or the groove
or the gear that powers the automaton.

A kite without wind has nothing
to lose. It will sprout fine legs
when it wants to move on.

Directive

I am working in a factory, day and night, just punching out
grail after grail, which makes them exceedingly
hard to see amidst so much sameness, same
glint along the handles, same fruited-vines and fluted edges,
same profusion of lyric orchids—molded pewter, every one. And dull.
Even when new. I wouldn't make them like that,
given half a chance. I'd go home
and plan it all out.

My first grail I would cut from paper,
to get a clearer sense of its edges. (You can't see a true grail
directly.) The second I would call from water—
to simulate a razzle-dazzle texture —something opaque
that bursts into light, like a snowflake slipping
from frost to crystal.

But the third grail—I can't
quite yet imagine. But it feels like impatience, skirmish,
freefall, and clangor; a listening like mist,
a many branched voice in the attic, electric allure—raw
steam crowned in radio static—
all singing something that can't be discerned
or dismissed.

Stand back. Observe.
The dreamer ascends from the ditch.

The Winch

In another kingdom, there is a winch.
I've heard it. It is ancient
with longing. Things
are rising and lowering on ropes
            black with age.
The things raised are piled by dusty beams,
            close to the ceiling.
They are given no sky.
The things lowered come to rest on the ocean floor
            to meld into rust.
They are given no air.
Everywhere, a stifling sameness. Everywhere,
the weeping of the winch.

Outside, an apple-green wind fills with kites and fans.

Another Sort of Time

For Erica (1951–2018)

After the scorched buildings cool,
after the tambourine lies battered among the bones
after the drowned all rise from the sea and cover the sea like lilies,
and all goodness fails,
after cruelty plants and harvests its iron baubles,
after Doomsday itself finishes off with a flourish—
will come a time
unlike the other times,
when Madness gently calms herself with grammar
and the Irrational sits down to knit strange glaring sweaters
that will be used as a system of laws in another time zone,
and Libraries dedicate themselves to healing—
and even after that

there will be a table

like anybody's table,
a table named "All That's Good Completes Us,"
revolving in a space of peace and plenty—
to remind all worlds there could be such a table.
That's where, my sweet, we'll drink black tea once more,
sharing our simple, ample, lazy breakfast—

And we will be the emblem of all friendships,
and all the living and all the dead skimming in rings around us will marvel
at the strength of such a friendship:

Division?
—We cannot be divided.
Confusion?
—Has often been our playground.
Sorrow?
—The underside of laughter.
Apocalypse?
—A fruit fly mired in ointment.
And the hour of death?—

the hour of *your* death,
which I have witnessed?

Dark waters lift the fullness of the lily.

Metamorphosis

If I could spend a week wandering through blossoming orchards,
I could change. I would sense things before they come
into view. I would draw what I need from the earth.

My skin would be bark, my bark would be vision and radiance,
and I would learn to see as the apple sees, inward,
inward, down into the core of things, down into the light
at the heart of sorrow, and further to the world's first living seed,
Where no one
         is left out.

Shapeshifter

This tree, this
injured tree, from blossoms
has learned the word "profusion,"
has dreamed herself a coastline and a password.
She loves speed.
Against a gray sky,
she is drinking wind and light. Soon
she will dream into cherries, ripples, full sail confusions of signposts,
the blighted leaf, and the dappled path. She will walk
as winter's skeleton among us, touching
her cranberry colored scarves.
Her hands are youthful.
Her ring finger's bone.
Hope is like that, sometimes.
Fear is like that . . .

Sheela Na Gig

"Why do you sit here, alone and solitary?
"I am not alone, I am on a journey."

~ From the life of a desert mother
whose name I have forgotten.

She is alone.
She is on a journey

Carved of stone,
on a wall by a well,
she is all alone.
She is mostly skull.
Her ribs descend here, bone by bone. The panic
is not hers alone: The panic has
          a tale to tell.

She is not alone.
She is on a journey.

She bears what must be borne, alone.
She bears alive what must be born.
The open diamond of her thighs,
the empty lantern of her chest—
such openings
          have a tale to tell.

She is not alone.
She is on a journey.

Life History

Back when we were young,
when there was no weather
but love, when those we loved shone
like constellations, like dragons
rising in splendor from sheathes of water
to join us on land, back when anything
could ripen—laughter
into sunburst, carole into compass, madrigals to fortress, silence
into slim swift ships—we said,

"Why *not* love the sudden storm?
Why not walk the world—hip, spine, and ditch?—
and down, through rippled, ribboned layers and up
upon the yodeling spires, then—
out of reach?"

Days spread. The slow vines bend.
Our fields lay rich around us.
Yet something within starves for deeper night.
And a wild and sudden ripening.

River Enough

I've been river enough to watch what arrives,
and regal enough to take what is given.

The burning log knows my name,
though I hid it deeper
than hunger.

And I know trouble well enough to wash its socks—
if I want to.

I'm moonlit most mornings.
—I find my way.

I have stories I can wear like tunics, variants like chariots, and rumors
loose as sleeves.

Write me backwards?
                    I will not vanish.
Short my shrift?
                    I'll speak with caves.

I'm demon enough to name my desires,
and omen enough to paint wings on stone.
I can hold my space—I can overflow it:

I've danced out of my slippers
—lots of times.

ALBRECHT CLASSEN

Dawn

Dreamy shadows
loom in figures
bizarrely.
My self revolves
restlessly
in delusion of existence,
inescapable
caught in a land
full of
syllogisms.
Growing fears
weave a net
of silvery dreams
around me in sleep,
clouding my last
rationality.
And then a blast
in endless night.

The Crane

A silver crane
touched my eyes
with its fragile wings
- while I was asleep -
gracefully
in a fleeting moment.
It whispered magic words
into my silent ears
and I slept
dreaming of past times
when truth was mine.
I smiled and listened
from the far distance
happy about those words.
But the crane flew away,
left it all up to me -
and then I was reborn.

Mysticism

Who would even know
what mystery meant
for the mystics
during the Middle Ages?
Magisterially
managed Hildegard
of Bingen,
managed Mechthild,
then also Catherine and Bridget
overcoming the mediocrity
of their masters' teachings,
challenging all limits,
breaking through the glass ceiling
of male concepts
about God.

Manifestations
of myriads
of visions
made it possible
for those mystics
to transcend
their mundane existence
and to get to know God
in the milieu
of their minuscule souls.

Kalamazoo

Graciously
the gods granted me
to fly in first class
after Kalamazoo.
Red wine
glass after glass,
and impeccable service,
I must have done something right,
and perhaps
this was the reward
for a decent paper?

Days of meetings
with colleagues
old and new,
some whom I met
more than thirty years ago,
some very young and brilliant,
time is really fleeting,
just look at my grey hair.

New theses tried out,
new arguments proposed,
new interpretations,
I know, I know,
maybe I just let it go.
We all have searched

for our pathways,
of tears and happy smiles.

And then, once again,
another book publication
to fill the crammed book shelves
with further and further ideas.
There is a whole universe
demanding ever new answers

for questions old and true.

Perhaps we should return to the mystics
freely flowing and unconstrained.
What did Tauler have to say,
and Rolle, not to disdain?
Margery's tears continue to flow,
how do we respond to her cries?

I, the Foreigner

Where are you from,
I mean, really, where are you from?
Tell me, I want to know,
where were you born,
where does your accent come from?

Why are you here?
where have you come from?
Why have you come here,
and where will you go?
You are welcome here,
for now, you know,
but I hope you will not stay.

Strangers united,
in a strange land,
multilingualists
and multireligionists,
multiethnics,
foreigners
in the same land.

Dear neighbor,
your accent
gives you also away,
maybe Scottish,
maybe Thai,

what did your grandfather do,
and who brought you here?

The tsunami of history
throws us all over the world,
from continent to continent,
dreaming of some happiness,
and this in the foreign land.

The wheel of fortune
turns incessantly,
and then Africa
might be the new fatherland
in the unknown tomorrow.

Medieval Individual

Sainthood
and dreamland
of past days.
Class structures
made it all easy
for people united in humankind.

Castles and fortresses
ruled over the lands
topping the mountains
like eagle nests
of a warrior society
submissive only to God.

Love and game
in front of hot fires.
Bitter coldness
in the rest of the rooms.
Oh, cursed winter
Oh, glorious spring.

Coats of arms
blazoned the men.
Dazzling beauty
adorned the women.
Color worship
in dreary worlds.

But they dreamt
and fancied
cried and laughed.
They loved and hated
fought and sang
strange medieval individual.

Our Dream

We were born
to live
and not to die.

We were born
to conquer
and not to be defeated.

We were born
to fulfill our dreams
and not see them fail.

We were born
to give love lavishly
and not to hate.

We were born
to create new life
and thus to live forever.

We were born
to see happiness bloom
and to dry the tears on your face.

We were born
and we will die
having lived a full life.

at night

Words and dreams
in nights
of light sleep,
of pictures
from afar,
are loopholes
leading outside
of ourselves
beyond language
deep into space
of life.

The weight
of earth
and death
stays behind
in the flight
from yesterday
to our tomorrow,
to love aspired
within and without
for all on earth.
We dream
and know,
we search
for new words
not based in language,
for life
not based in life,
for knowledge
not based in knowledge,
for love
not based in love.

The answer
resonates
in the fugue,

it rings
so deeply
in the sonata,
in pearls
and corals,
it whispers
in the clouds
among the leaves
and deeply in the sea.

unnamed

Salt of life
and bitterness of gall
pain of death
experiences of loss
night follows day
the young grow old
and then the end.
Sugar of life
results
from our pain
the day returns
after each night
the loss makes room
for ever new growth
our tears will soak
a fertile soil
fear not the dark
it stands at the cradle
of all our light.

THOM FOY

Love is a Bubble

that stretches and grows.
But many are repelled
by its rubbery surface.
We inside
must reach out
and populate Love.
Together in liquid emotion
We seek
the distilled Life.

When the Sun Rises in the Morning

When the sun rises in the morning, I
am there to see it. First the Sky is
black, then a sultry blue. Like Lovers
finally asleep in each other's arms
the pale light of morning makes its
presence known: orange clouds streak
the Sky; the color of blue is now
vibrant. How wonderful is that blend
of blue and orange! Our Lovers are
together again in each other's Dreams
but soon They will wake as the play-
fulness of the early morning Sky is
replaced by a solid blue, the color
of Love.

Christmas Eve

Christmas eve in the middle of the
night I woke up and looked out
the window. I saw God Peacefully
resting on the blue midnight snow.

I became aware of all the people
living and all the people dead, and
of all those not yet born. That night
was the longest night of my
Life. God was showing me Heaven.

In the morning, I awoke to a day like no other in the year.

Turning

It used to be more touchable, reachable.
It was colorful and vibrant
Its life was full and throbbing.

But it has begun to fade
Taking on a grayish grainy hue.
Its inhabitants' joints have seized a bit,

Their movements greatly slowed.
There is a nephew on the floor
Toward whom mother turns,

A sister at the sink.
The orange carpet, the counter, and the dark brown cabinets
Form a familiar stain within me.

I miss especially my mother,
There in that kitchen.
She is turning, and her hair is dark.

Her hair is as dark as it is now white
(It is far from center, which is me).
She can't turn quite as fast because of her joints—

joints of 50 years—But she smiles.
The smile is constant, enduring, unending and
transcends time, beauty, this life.

It beams from that everlasting kitchen like God's love.
Like the Second Coming.
Like Christmas.

Transgression

At his end, excruciating yellow; an overexposed photo; aperture full open.
While here, dusty white mini-blinds alternate sunlight and shadow on my chest.
Peering through the light I exercise a great power of perception,
staring down the gaze of my age.

Looking through the wrong end of a telescope;
he's just a dot, but he's there, standing where I am now.
He's doing what I am doing right now:
staring, squinting, straining.

As the strain grips us both we seem to squirt out of our skins,
careen down the long tube of the telescope
and graze each other
lightly, gently, halfway through.

We fondle the solidity of each other's profundity—
the beings of our nothingnesses—
and know a oneness that transcends time.
We wonder at the linkage that connects us all.

It's there that some cosmic force—an eternal sentinel, Einstein's secret police—
shuffles us back to where we came from, our respective ghettoes.
(We'll be together again, we whisper to ourselves, each other,
while the dust floats in the light, never to settle, never to rest.)

The Quiet King

(1 Kings 19: 11-13)

I stood on the summit
        waiting for God,
when a great and mighty wind came
        and shook the mountain.
But God was not in the wind.

Then the earth quaked
        and shattered the rocks.
But God was not in the quake.
        And a fire came,
but God was not in the fire.

Then as I stared
        into the mouth of the cave,
the last stones tinkling into silence,
the last charred stick cracking,
        extinguished,
a gentle whisper, so still and so small,
        Spoke.

Sweltering: Two Views

Alpha:
Long ago
left among the flowers and trees,
It leaves a snail trail
crossing the autumn leaves of my mind.
This perennial huckster of springtime
grows death in its garden of pain.

Omega:
Leading on, the whore,
        she leads her train, infants
in Eternity. Brazen, she, her
charges march an infant's two-step
waddle—their eyes cut, bleeding
transparent blood. She leads them,
legions, leagues, leaving them
to bathe in the warm viscous
ejaculate of her bowl which,
cascading thickly from a great height,
creates a translucent curtain across
        the world.

The Tender

He lived in this glorious world,
where great vibrations rippled through him
and music pervaded the sky.
He watched the clouds and heard them speak.
He saw birds come in and out of his mind.
He felt wisdom in its place and easy.
He knew you and he knew me and he was there,
always there, never leaving.

All was well and all was easy; but he worked,
worked hard and he maintained this world and the peace
for years and years and years...

The Ease of a Sunday Walk in Winter

You are the gentle ease
of a Sunday in Winter.

Softly you
touch my cheek
as I walk
across the snow
covering the yard.

And you are in
the color
of the snow—
a reflection
of the pensive
gray sky—
and in its
comforting crunch—
(something like the
stroke stroke swish
of father shaving in the morning
as I drifted back from sleeping).

I seek you
among the apple trees
and cherry trees
and blueberries.
As I walk
your powder wake
waves across my boots
and settles again,
unflapped,
despite the row
of holes I've left
in your blanket.

You are with me
and in me

as I walk
among the stones
of your temple.
I close in
on your many parts
and you yield,
easily, knowingly,
with a wisdom
that balances your submission.

The veins of a leaf,
the touch of a snowflake,
the aroma of the air—
the cold air and the quiet . . .
Isolation
makes beautiful
those things
which the crowd
often swallows
in its noisy swath across time.

You are the pervasive
unending quiet
that underlies it all.
You've come to me
again after a long absence
and I am eternally grateful.

KATHARINE JAGER

The Word Hoard is Enormous

Tree's in the kitchen mulling over crock-pot
cookery, meals for loss and love and patience,
when I interrupt to say I've found *honypot*
and *honydere* in Chaucer. Also *cleve* and *swyve,*
swynke, coke, starf and *clem. Clem?* she
asks and I say *starf. Swyve* and *swynke* are *screw* and *toil.*
Every word's a string
of sound for what it is we really mean
to say. The Miller's Alison's a *weasel,*
swallow, ragdoll, colt. She's a *primerole,*
a *piggesnye.* And Tree's not *Tree* but *Jennifer,* who sits
considering casseroles, chrysanthemums, and New York flights
to Cape Town for a newborn's funeral.

That small girl was so new we never knew
her name. She won't grow into appellation's grace,
won't be given nicknames. The word hoard is
enormous, a slipping solace of noise
and sense, but nothing, I know,
neither elegy nor recipe, really lessens
sorrow's grasp. There's little that can carry us
across that awful slough of grief but time.

Recuperation and Recitation:
The General Prologue

It's less the tender crops. Rather, birdsong.
The starlings colonize our pediment,

make shit-smeared holes in the acanthus leaf
that scrolls the tenement roofline. When fledged,

those gawpers hit the blue-bagged Times that waits
each morning on the threshold. Then, they die.

O harbingers of spring! Every vein's bathed
in solar succor. All windows opened!

I wait and sleep and read. Avian breasts,
those courageous hearts, are pricked to action.

To prick's to stick, to poke, to course along,
a knight errant and a needle, the quest

to find a target. The nurse says, "Now you'll
feel a pinch," euphemism for the prick

of metal entering the body.
Sharp, actual pain. NPR mutters

from Iraq, the reporter talking men
and insurrection, "bodies showing signs

of torture." Euphemism for
drill bit to the temple. Beyond his voice, doves

are making melody in the date palm.
He does not acknowledge their brief lyric,

their breaking through the news. It's April.
The small fowls call, from Brooklyn to Baghdad.

Scent and Bestiary

One jar of yellow freesia swamps the house—
redolent and delicate conjurer,
these gathered stalks recall stillettoed girls
out walking cloistered filthy cobblestones,
their swathed and powdered necks clouded with silk,
with perfume so perfect a mimicry
it seemed they were crowned with flowers. Alcohol
and oil laden ions swung from their hair,
from their sweated pulse-points. My beloved,
in foreign cities I could find you by
your throat's aroma alone, our filial
meldings spent in webs of scent.
A stem of petals is a reliquary,
is our mute thread to the bestiary.

For the Makaris (after Palestrina)

To the clarified realm of passion let us comeaway,
my love, my fair one. Let us press
our bodies each to each. Match
the navel's smooth goblet, pair up the anointed heart
to its fellow, bleating and surging there
in an opposite
palace of bone. Let us sound out longing, lost
summer lambs amidst the fells. Then let the intellect
drop its scrim of speech
to reveal an elegant hunger, this swell
of scent and song and longing, all that precedes us. Our
melody's
antiphony, the want in me sending out
its delicate arc
to find the want in you, expansive, generous, and all the while
crying: join me,
join me, in the very cleft of what we make, let us rise
up, my love, into a coupled newness, our name
like a perfume poured out,
O *my chiefest*
of ten thousand, let us be joined
on this verdant bed,
for lo, the winter is past, the rain is over and gone.

Renaissance Technology

Piero della Francesco's triumph
was perspective, geometry's secret:
how to render the Holy form in three

complete dimensions. So when Christ steps down,
in this spacious Baptism, He casts off
the gold leaf environs of paradise,

the alien faces of the triptych.
He enters the pastoral's mathematic
order, and one could say that He has found

us. Behind His cocked right hip sits Piero's
Sansepolcro, little hill town, its red-
roofed towers and ochre plaster cupolas

chaotic and toppling in miniature
detail, and, at the river's bend, a man
who lifts his shift to reveal underthings

even we would recognize, preparing
himself for St. John's promise. The static
angels stare in laurel-crowned astonishment.

The hills are each isosceles triangles.
Christ's contraposto, a classic curved weight,
He's as slender as the beech beside Him.

And the foreshortened dove, new birth's guide,
hovers above the gold bowl. She is a cross
of white wings, herald of what's yet to come.

The Dragon

Saint Margaret is the girl who covers birth.
Patroness of all women bearing down,
those blown open by another's body,
her body flayed and seared, the blood that flowed
copiously, sickening onlookers
who counseled she accept her tormentor,
give up on her virginity, give in
and live. The saint chose suffering, the cell,
the iron-fanged dragon burst by the cross
he'd swallowed in swallowing her. No child
ever fought for space amidst her organs.
She never woke to wailing fragile need,
but served in death *that sovereign godhead*
that has preserved my maidenhead so far.

Varieties of Religious Experience

A man in Plain can pass
as Hasid, though his hat lacks a Satmar's
beaver pelted finery. The beard and

flat collared shirt hail him as another
believer dressed in simple proof of his
devotion. But were I to don the bonnet,

grab the pinafore about me, go free
of the usual adornments, I'd be
the shock of the canned goods aisle. I'd be

that girl in the niqab at Starbucks
fumbling with her cotton gloved hands to tear
sugar packets, her mouth invisible,

taken out of social circulation.
The patrons pitied her, smugly muttered
her father had forced her into that shroud,

someone hissed *oppression*. No one can believe
a woman might decide, like Julian
of Norwich, to hear the offices

of the dead read above her bent prayer
as masons bricked the anchorhold, that she
might choose the hot cover of God's clear love.

Legenda Aurea

No Catholic, I lacked a book of saints,
had instead her sad story of marrying bad,
that angry Irishman who used his fists.
No matter. You married whom you married
and if you divorced, the bonneted aunts
kept the visit to the porch. I doubt she drank,
though he did, and of course there were no cards,
no dancing. Just coal dust wrung in washtubs.
For years I thought only idolaters
got more than an orange at Christmas, but
what she withheld was more convention than
belief. She was pregnant when they wed, then
left Meeting and her parents' tidy farm.
He hit her. Their first of three girls was born.

Iona

Columcille, your sealskin coracle
pitch-daubed and leaking brine, left death behind
to find a marble-pebbled bay, the sun
refracted past the heather and the fern.

When you landed were there yews yet standing?
The coral light and water, yellow gorse,
the knotted cross, granite for your pillow.
You sang matins, made the two a.m. upright

shuffling through the grass and graves, to reach
the altar with a mouth of psalms. A certain
loneliness obtained. Weasels ate gull eggs.
The shrike cried and the kestrel. There was no

peat to burn and soon enough no timber.
But you wrote and then were written of,
streaks of oak gall, flourishes, the gold leaf
fixed by glue and static to the parchment

that would one day bear your name. Columba,
little dove of Christ, your heart each morning
turned to face the dawn, away from home,
and hopeful for the writing to get done.

A.J. ODASSO

Prosthetics

We put on dresses Sunday morning,
our private joke. Old friends will
want to see us at church. Mom says
it's really nice to have us home.

I know the nearness now
of death, and your brave face
feels like a punch-line. We sit
through Sacrament still as saints.

After bread and water, after talks
that set my Jewish teeth on edge
and you to drawing on your arm,
we endure handshakes. Glassy

smiles reflect what I know
better than to suspect: all eyes
low, lashes frown. We flee
before Second Hour sends

invitations to scripture study
our way. We take Mom's car,
zip to Sheetz, order hot dogs
with chili, onion, and cheese.

Some drops right on my chest.
You laugh, say there's nothing
left to catch it. I think about
those pious, lowered eyes

and puzzled smiles. You say
you remember the location
of that creepy cabin filled
with dozens of fake arms

and ancient newsprint. I say
I'd like to see it. You drive

through drizzle a little while
till the dirt road rises. Gladly

I'd have struck out through trees
to hunt this slumber-party legend,
but we stare through the fog-slick
windshield. My twin scars ache.

Maybe next time we'll try
trespassing, you say. I nod,
chewing in silence. We go on,
watching for deer in the rain.

Cruel Sister, Revised

after several Child Ballads

No undead harp for stringing:
neither you, nor I. My heart
has ferried yours these five
and twenty years gone

so the river cannot
claim us. The miller's
daughter becomes me:
swan-kind, blue-garbed

instead. The red, you see,
is in my hair. None ever
sang she had a sister, too,
but discord is the music's

undoing: cry murder; cry
false, false! The truest
have you been of all fair
yarrow, darling child, but

our once-upon-a-times burn
contrariwise: mercy isn't for
the likes of love unspoiled.
The breastbone harp lies.

The Recto Fragments

FOR SALE: Two pages from a French prayer-book, ca. 1420
folio 31

Draw me in, blue-veiled beauty. Your tears
singe my skin: this heart can feel again

in spite of the dust that confounds me.
I've been sick to death's brink, senses dulled

by the promise of wellness. It takes years,
so turn the page / set the clock / halt the spell

of ink-blot poison in my veins. His skin
a tracery of rust-tracks and thorn, his ears

deaf shells a-ring with mourning. His eyes.

Yours.

•

folio 180
Did you not die already?

I saw—
the shroud, the tomb. The wounds
unburdened of blood. Wings

in the webbing
of your hair. Your mother
made round, low sounds

like a [quill-scraped] bird

or—

a [salt-stained] fish. Shrubs
in the distance. Barrow-mounds
of sand, the Dead Sea.

Your drying wish.

Hers.

Origin Story

Each death
a mirror:

teeth shed,
skin torn.

Each fin
an eddy:

etched,
unshorn.

Monster,
you call me.

I swim
farther

from shore.

The Breakers Fail

Cyclone-sighted,
cataclysmic:

my gaze, you said,
summoned storms

on the Atlantic.
Leviathan land-

locked, whirlpool
in human skin.

One year gone,
the day I tore

your net. Desert-
brash, my scales

glint with plunder
I clawed back.

You fade iron-
haired, tide-choked

for monstrous lack.

DNR

I am so thin, reads the mimeograph, final line
in my great-grandmother's letter. Records say
it was consumption that killed her, slow wasting-
away of hunger and breath. *I am so thin*, she says
again, her last graphite-scrawl a repetition.

•

I have known fever, fire gone viral in my blood
after swift incubation. H1N1-haunted dreams
raised my temp to a hundred and three. I lay
raving for days while the NHS Direct hotline
told my partner to keep me warm. *I think I'm
dying*, I rasped, grabbing the phone. *I'm afraid.*

•

Clean typeface in lieu of scrawling, nib-fine
ascenders scaffold a loved-one's living will.
Do not resuscitate, it says, deceptively brief
with dotted I and curly-crossed *Ts. We are so
thin*, I think, signing the paper. *We are so thin.*

Haunting Harvard Square

Grief grow gaunt, and breath
blow still. Leaves, new brightness
in the shivering, silvering green
are all I can ask. Stay a while
with me here if you can. Let's pass
from rusted lock to riverbed
under cloud-bled blue: no chance
will steer us from the path
on which we're set. One heel
ahead of the other, your ghost
just a step behind. Red Line
to the right of us, Charles tide-
line to the left. Only you
know where we're going,
fierce-footed even in death.

Timepiece

You put your watch—
worn, Timex, cheap—
in my hand. I was nine.
You said, "Listen,
those oil drums behind
the garage are about
to blow." The coil of
my digits unwound.
I was nine. You said,
"Lit trash fell out-
side the burn barrel.
The oil will catch.
Get your brother
and your sisters
in the car." I was
nine. And you said,
"I'm going back. I'll
try to put it out. Get
the kids in the car
and drive if I don't
come back." But Dad,
you did. Every word,
each tick. We lived.

Treasure

Silk from a sow's ear,
you called me once—

No Miss America,
but smart as fuck.

Three pretty sisters
obscured my looks.

The middle pair, you loved
passing well. The youngest,

you touched like chattel
while she fixed her hair.

Silk from a sow's ear,
you called me once.

My mouth spills coins,
a hangman's purse.

KATHERINE DURHAM OLDMIXON (GARZA)

Crossing

"May I for my own self song's truth reckon"
~ *The Seafarer*

Always warm winter   in these wastelands
far from their fallow fields— they suffer no green-frost,
no wind shudders tender cactus blades clinging
hard to barbed arms   since the summer sun
               hung heavy in this dry heaven.

They pass a sepia gecko stirring sand,
spreading the shallows of Gulf silt,
oil swirls and arcs on wavering waters—
They hesitate where the honey-hymns
            of bees blear memory.

In the heat they dream their world wanders
among dust of dying day-stars
flashes of gun-silver   bloat-bellied fish,
sour wings of old raptors,
            cold-rasp coyote whispers

"Photographs of the Saint's Finger are Strictly Prohibited"

Convent of St. Teresa, Ávila, Spain

We have come to see the finger—
from her right hand, a roll of bony lace

at last at rest in its gold and glass glove
after lifelong journeys on a priest's breast—

now separate from her transverberated heart
and the arm they cut, after the finger,

revealing her body still uncorrupt
when it bled the medieval must of roses.

The church men sawed off a foot,
her other arm, a sliver of her jaw, bits

of flesh—there must be an inventory—
before they reburied what remained.

And here we are only for that finger
whose sometime tremble was, in their eyes,

the vital sign in her three-year coma. How
they must have watched it flicker on her bed

until it became the girl
and all the body they could bear.

Rites of St. Agatha

patron of volcanoes, bell makers, bread bakers and nurses
after *Saint Agatha* by Lorenzo Lippi, Florence, Italy 1606-1665

Agatha doesn't look at her severed breasts
or the hinged metal shears in her hands.

Resting on silver as if a delicate dessert,
two camellia-pink glands make a still life

you can't bear to glance at—though you do,
then to the touch of lace at her bodice, cleft

shadow and her face—tucked lower lip,
open-earth eyes—her curious gaze. You,

she watches as if she knows what you want
to know. You face a woman forced

from her body.
A body pushed out of language defies

meaning. Let no woman brush her hair;
let us bless the breads; may our bells sing.

How to Make a Palimpsest

before it was a metaphor

Scrape fat from the skin,
turn to the sun what never felt light,
in vitriol bathe open wounds,
sear the inner vellum
until flesh and hair transmute.
Fold quarto, fold folio;
make flocks of pages to lay in wait.

Sharpen a feather,
dip the shaft in iron gall.
Write angel-pin philosophy,
the brewer's daily tabs,
a festal grocery list, poems
and psalms for a choir gathered to praise
God. Until you think, no more:

Take a knife to dead hymns,
rub out names, cut leaves to strips,
tuck them in other spines,
wood or bone shells.
So buried is living in the skeletons
and tissues we open on cradles.

Saint Sebastian

after the painting by Guido Reni in the Huston Collection, Franciscan University of Steubenville

Guido, how many times did you imagine him?
No one could love that young man more than you.

Each time you stretched him on your dark canvas,
he seems more beautiful—his face, serene

after agony, the left leg, raised to relieve
pressure from the arrows under his breast,

a soft-knotted sheet laid over his pubic
bone (the white cloth's loose end left dangling)

rose light and shadow sculpting his flesh—
Then muscles you hadn't before considered the way

you would at last, when here in your full maturity,
you painted him differently, as a man of sinew,

wrists bound over his reclining body draped
in red rising to meet between his bare thighs.

Philomela

long after Ovid

I.

After a time it felt like my native tongue,
this split root. When my swallow sister

flew not too long afterwards, grieving her
child, she'd gathered every scrap in winter

into her nest. (What can I say but *what a mess?*)
Everywhere, bits and pieces and soft matter.

She starved at last, leaving all she had to me,
each morsel and eggshell.

II.

It's true I sang in their ears, each man who would
make me artful. All night perched in a cypress

outside a window, into a bedchamber
I poured my song like poison into the air

of a sleepless king or lured an aging poet
to cold, enameled gold and jeweled flesh,

or a young one to scribble crumbs for birds,
my voice a thread drawing them to my mouth.

III.

Here, you see: my lips sheathed in bone,
my sex downed over, my soft hands good

only for flying. Now I grow quills,
needles that pierce my skin and

darkness, closed lids, weave where I am
trapped again under his body, his fingers

pulling out my language, my shuttle
pressed into the dirt under my head.

IV.

Beneath dirt a wild man once dreamed
songless birds sojourned in the clay—

How I wish I could lay down this lyric,
ravel my story and weave the threads

into a turquoise shawl, pink booties,
slipcovers for the dining room chairs.

Adivina

At Córdoba, when the Mezquita casts no shadows,
in the temple doorway a woman handed me

a sprig of rosemary—*un regalo*, she assured
when I tried to pull away. *What is it?* I asked,

but she had me by the wrist, tracing
the lines in my palm incanting, *amor muy fuerte,*

inteligente, stroked my other hand, asking
in Spanish if I understood Spanish. I nodded,

entranced, but hearing only the music
of *niños* and *la persona mas importante, la vida*—

the reverence in her voice, I trusted.
When I heard her say, *accidente,* blood

rushed to my ears, drowning her
last instructions about burning or burying

the oily herb pressed in my flesh when it dries,
drowning my spirit, as I reached to hand her

ten euros. *Veinte,* she said, but walked away
as I shook my head, her spell joining

the ghosts of prayers pushing pagan pilgrims
into the sanctuary. I turned to wander

through the myriad arches of the dim interior,
trying not to talk out loud while trying to recall

what I hadn't heard, telling myself the truth:
it was a tourist scam. Why should I dread what I

hadn't understood, nothing to believe—but how
do you know what to believe or not in a mosque

that is a cathedral on the site of a Roman temple,
when you find your tongue incoherent, your map

confused in the city of Averroes and Maimonides—
or when a stranger appears to read your crazed skin?

Marina, La Malinche

I fold my tongue into a hollow reed.
I'm an amber butterfly pressed

into the neck of milkweed florets
dripping nectar through my waiting throat.

I push my tongue to palate, swallow
like a wood thrush gathering sand grit,

cry evensongs until the skin-pale moon
leaves our Mexican sky for another continent.

I roll my tongue like the snake below
the feathered body struggling to taste

dry desert air; I thread cactus spines to whet
native spirit or teach the mother tongue to pray;

I would hold my tongue, but must speak
to survive. My father sold me destined to lie

with a man who crossed our oceans to let blood
and tongues mingle. I keen lullabies.

Tonantzin, La Guadalupe de Juan Diego

after Tepeyac

In an aureole of gold flames, she wears
a veil of stars on a Mexican-blue sky,

its interior like rare grass, her robe spun
cotton of roses, and below her a man

with green wings clutches her gathering
hem, as he holds her above

a cupped crescent, sign of his native moon.
He bows his head, his vision cast down—

as her eyes, too, look away from him
and heaven. Once she spoke

to him in his Nahuatl tongue,
pressed her image into his tilma,

filled it with flowers. Her scent brought
a bishop to his knees. Yet they say

a woman is no god, only a human
sanctified by maternity, a saint

with no instrument of torture,
now or at the hour of our death.

ABOUT THE POETS

Jane Beal, PhD is chair of English and an associate professor of English at the University of La Verne in southern California. She is the author of many books of poetry, including *Sanctuary* (Finishing Line Press, 2008), *Rising* (Wipf and Stock, 2015), and *Song of the Selkie* (Aubade Publishing, forthcoming). She is also the creator of three recording projects combining music and poetry: "Songs from the Secret Life," "Love-Song," and with her brother, saxophonist and composer, Andrew Beal, "The Jazz Bird." Her poems appear widely in print, online, and in anthologies, including *New Crops from Old Fields: Eight Medievalist Poets* and *Hail, Radiant Star! Seven Medievalist Poets*, the latter of which she edited. She has produced seven academic books, including three on the medieval dream vision poem called *Pearl*: an academic monograph, *The Signifying Power of Pearl: Medieval Literary and Cultural Contexts for the Transformation of Genre* (Routledge, 2017); an edited collection of pedagogical essays, *Approaches to Teaching the Middle English Pearl* (MLA, 2017), and a dual-language edition-translation, *Pearl: A Middle English Edition and Modern English Translation* (Broadview, 2019). To learn more, see janebeal.wordpress. com.

Gail Ivy Berlin has poems published in *Lilliput Review, Poetry Depth Quarterly*, and the *New Growth Arts Review*. She attended Bread Loaf as a tuition scholar in poetry in the summer of 2016. Her poetry explores the mysterious interconnections between identity and transformation, past and present, the living and the dead, silence and the edges of language. She aims for a sense of expansion. Recently retired from Indiana University of Pennsylvania after a thirty-two year career, Gail has worked as a medievalist specializing in Old and Middle English language and literature and medieval women. Her publications include work on the Aesop's Fables in the margin of the Bayeux Tapestry, Moses in Middle English biblical literature, and Tonwenne's breast baring gesture in Laȝamon's *Brut*. Much of her current research deals with the *Brut*, and she enjoys placing particular episodes from this text within a cultural context. For this purpose, she has dealt with such topics as magic and gadgets, uroscopy, early attempts at flight, bridge sacrifice legends, and medieval ditches, all with equal joy.

Albrecht Classen is University Distinguished Professor of German Studies at the University of Arizona where he teaches and researches the European Middle Ages and early modern time. In his by now 96 scholarly books and ca.

640 articles, he has investigated a wide range of topics, including women in the pre-modern world, medieval ecocriticism, magic and science, friendship, urban and rural space, multilingualism, mental health and hygiene, crime and punishment, war and peace, and communication. He is the editor of the journals *Mediaevistik* and *Humanities Open Access*. He has received numerous awards for his teaching, research and academic service. Most recently, he received the rank of Grand Knight Commander of the Most Noble Order of the Three Lions (GCTL). He is also an accomplished poet, having published nine volumes of his own, and close to individual 150 poems in various journals and magazines.

Thom Foy's poetical interests are far reaching, always striving for the infinite within human thought, mediated by language. He teaches writing and rhetoric at the University of Michigan-Dearborn. His research interests include medieval romance and metaphysics as well as adaptation. Since 2014, he has adapted and performed several of Tolkien's works for reader's theater at the International Congress on Medieval Studies in Kalamazoo, Michigan, and at the 2017 Congress, he staged his adaptation of Tolkien's "Leaf by Niggle." He enjoys his family and his students, and he also finds joy in the solitude of running and the fellowship of travel.

Katharine Jager is a poet and a medieval scholar. She is associate professor of English at the University of Houston-Downtown, and has published poetry in *Before the Door of God: An Anthology of Lyric Devotional Verse* (Yale); *The Gettysburg Review; Found; Canteen; Friends Journal; The Great River Review;* and *GoodFoot* among other journals. She has an MFA from New York University.

A.J. Odasso's poetry has appeared in a variety of publications, including *Sybil's Garage, Mythic Delirium, Midnight Echo, Not One of Us, Dreams & Nightmares, Goblin Fruit, Strange Horizons, Stone Telling, Farrago's Wainscot, Liminality, Battersea Review, Barking Sycamores,* and *New England Review of Books*. A.J.'s début collection, *Lost Books* (Flipped Eye Publishing), was nominated for the 2010 London New Poetry Award and was also a finalist for the 2010/2011 People's Book Prize. A second collection with Flipped Eye, *The Dishonesty of Dreams*, was released in 2014; a third-collection manuscript, *Things Being What They Are*, was shortlisted for the 2017 Sexton Prize. A.J. holds an M.F.A. in Creative Writing from Boston University, where A.J. was a 2015-16 Teaching Fellow, and A.J. has worked at the University of New Mexico. A.J. has served in the Poetry Department at *Strange Horizons* magazine (www.strangehorizons.com) since July 2012.

Katherine Durham Oldmixon (Garza) is the author of *Water Signs*, finalist for the New Women's Voices Award (Finishing Line Press, 2009). Her poems and photographs appear in many print and online journals, such as *Borderlands: Texas Poetry Review, Solstice Literary Magazine, The Bellevue Review, The Normal School, Sequestrum, Minerva Rising, the Cider Press Review, Mom Egg Review*, and the anthologies *Improbable Worlds: An Anthology of Texas and Louisiana, Lifting the Sky: Southwestern Haiku and Haiga, Bearing the Mask: Persona Poems of the Southwest*, and *Red Sky: Poetry on the Global Epidemic of Violence Against Women*. Katherine holds a Ph.D. in English from UT-Austin, where she wrote her dissertation on the Middle English Breton Lays. She earned her MFA in creative writing from University of New Orleans, and an M.A., with a concentration in medieval folklore, from University of Houston. Co-director of the Poetry at Round Top festival, Katherine is professor and chair of English at historic Huston-Tillotson University in Austin, TX.

www.ingramcontent.com/pod-product-compliance
Lightning Source LLC
Chambersburg PA
CBHW021149090426
42740CB00008B/1013